———————— ◇ ————————

Once Upon a Christmas

Compiled & edited by
Emilie Griffin

Illustrated by
Barbara Wilson

The C.R. Gibson Company, Norwalk, CT 06856

Preface

As a child I was deeply stirred by the words, "Once upon a time." It was not merely because they were spoken with loving voices, the same voices that sang me to sleep and tucked me in with tender hands. There was more to it than the context that cradled me. The depth of those fairy-tale words spoke to me of something true, kindled yearnings for a was-and-would-be time, a kingdom I could almost remember but not name.

Christmas — and the days before and after — are celebrations of that yearning, our heart's cry for fulfillment and peace. When we have lived long enough that earthly peace seems a mockery and promise another word for heartache, Christmas calls us to hope: for truth, beauty, holiness and celebration.

In these pages, then, a circle of writers calling ourselves the Chrysostom Society, weaves garlands of civility to celebrate the season. Calling on imaginative resources, we make tapestries from the shreds and patches of our experience. Something learned in the womb of memory is born again in us, a childhood spirit of peace-making and simplicity, of harmony and hope.

Welcome gentle readers to this once-and-forever moment. May this little book bring you Christmas in all its royal splendor, told afresh with all the wondering, wandering joy of our raggle-taggle group. It is a time for living, a time for forgiveness and laughter, for wolves to lie with the lambs, for cows and bears to be friends, *"Once upon a Christmas..."*

Emilie Griffin
Editor

Contents

Our House is Open – Luci Shaw   6

Announcement – Luci Shaw   7

This Gloriously Impossible Baby – Madeleine L'Engle   8

It is as if infancy were the whole of incarnation – Luci Shaw   10

The Christmas Story – Walter Wangerin, Jr.   12

Christmas Prayer – John Leax   15

Star Song – Luci Shaw   16

Letter to Friends-Advent, 1990 – John Leax   18

Chance – Luci Shaw   20

The Adoration of the Magi – Madeleine L'Engle   22

A Celibate Epiphany – Luci Shaw   24

Vigil: Christmas Eve, 1991 – John Leax   26

Small Gifts – Karen Burton Mains   27

Our Lady of I-80 – Calvin Miller   32

A Victorian Plum Pudding – Barbara Miller   34

Wassail Bowl – Barbara Miller   36

The Secret Stair – Shirley Nelson   37

One Night Only/Handel's Messiah – Philip Yancey   48

The Twelve Days of Christmas – Eugene Peterson   53

Under the Snowing – Luci Shaw   65

Christmas Eve – Robert Siegel   66

Hopkins, Skipkins & Jumpkins – William Griffin   67

The Holy Child – Emilie Griffin   77

A Psalm at the Sunrise – Walter Wangerin, Jr.   82

Poems by Calvin Miller   85

ur house is open, Lord, to thee;
Come in, and share our Christmas tree!
We've made each nook and corner bright,
Burnished with yellow candle-light.

But light that never burns away
Is only thine, Lord Jesus. Stay,
Shine on us now, our Christmas Cheer—
Fill with thy flame our whole New Year!

Luci Shaw

Announcement

Luci Shaw

Yes we have seen the studies, sepia strokes
across yellowed parchment, the fine detail
of hand and breast and the fall of cloth—
Michelangelo, Caravaggio, Titian, El Greco,
Rouault—each complex Madonna positioned,
sketched, enlarged, each likeness plotted at last
on canvas, layered with pigment, like the final
draft of a poem after thirty-nine roughs.

But Mary, virgin, had no sittings, no chance
to pose her piety, no novitiate for body or
for heart. The moment was on her unaware:
the Angel in the room, the impossible demand,
the response without reflection. Only one
word of curiosity, echoing Zechariah's How?
yet innocently voiced, without request for proof.
The teen head tilted in light, the hand
trembling a little at the throat, the candid
eyes, wide with acquiescence to shame and glory—
"Be it unto me as you have said."

The Gloriously Impossible Baby

Madeleine L' Engle

And so he was born, this gloriously impossible baby, in a stable in Bethlehem. Mary and Joseph had to leave home because of the general census ordered by Rome; so Joseph took his young, pregnant wife to register in Bethlehem, because he was of the house of David.

Little Bethlehem was crowded, overcrowded with people coming to register. There was no room in the inn, no place for Joseph to take Mary, whose labor was beginning. How terrifying for Mary to be wracked with pain while Joseph tried helplessly to find someplace for them to stay. Finally they were guided to a cave where animals were lodged. There Mary gave birth to the infant Jesus, surrounded by lowing cattle, by donkeys and oxen. Exhausted, but filled with joy, she laid him in a manger.

Nearby, some shepherds were out in a field with their flocks when suddenly an angel of the Lord appeared before them and the glory of the Lord shone brilliantly all around them. And they were terrified.

"Fear Not!" the angel cried, and told them of the birth of the child who would bring joy to all people. They were told that they would find this holy child wrapped in linen cloths and lying in a manger.

Suddenly the angel was surrounded by a host of heavenly angels, singing in a mighty chorus to the glory of God.

When the angels left and the shepherds were able to speak, they hurried to Bethlehem. There they found Mary and Joseph, just as the angel had said, and the baby lying in a manger. They told Mary and Joseph about the angels, and Mary listened and treasured their words. Gently the shepherds placed simple gifts — a lamb, a woolen wrap, a ball— by the baby and then Mary and Joseph were left alone with the child, marveling.

Holding the child in her arms, rocking, singing, Mary wondered what was going to happen to him, this sweet innocent creature who had been conceived by the incredible love of God and who had been born as all human babies are born.

God, come to be one of us.

It is as if infancy were the whole of incarnation

Luci Shaw

*One time of the year
the new–born child
is everywhere,
planted in madonnas' arms
hay mows, stables,
in palaces or farms,
or quaintly, under snowed gables,
gothic angular or baroque plump,
naked or elaborately swathed,
encircled by Della Robbia wreaths,
garnished with whimsical
partridges and pears,
drummers and drums,
lit by oversize stars,
partnered with lambs,
peace doves, sugar plums,
bells, plastic camels in sets of three
as if these were what we need
for eternity.*

*But Jesus the Man is not to be seen.
We are to be wary, these days,
of beards and sandalled feet.*

Yet if we celebrate, let it be
that He
has invaded our lives with purpose,
striding over our picturesque traditions,
our shallow sentiment,
overturning our cash registers,
wielding His peace like a sword,
rescuing us into reality,
demanding much more
than the milk and the softness
and the mother warmth
of the baby in the storefront creche,
(only the Man would ask
all, of each of us)
reaching out
always, urgently, with strong
effective love
(only the Man would give
His life and live
again for love of us).

Oh come, let us adore Him—
Christ—the Lord.

The Christmas Story

Walter Wangerin, Jr.

And there were shepherds in that same dark country, abiding in the fields, keeping watch over their flocks by night.

And God turned to his angel. And God said, "Gabriel."

And the angel answered, "Yes, Lord?"

And the Lord God said, "Go down. All of the people must know what I am doing. Tired and lonely and scattered and scared, all of the people must hear it. Go, good Gabriel. Go down again. Go tell a few to tell the others, till every child has heard it. Go!"

And so it was that an angel of the Lord appeared to the weary shepherds. Their dark was shattered, for the glory of the Lord shone round about them, and they were sore afraid.

The angel said to them, "Don't be afraid."

But the light was like a hard and holy wind, and the shepherds shielded their faces with their arms.

"Hush," said the angel, "hush," like the west wind. "Shepherds, I bring you good news of great joy, and not only for you but for all of the people. Listen."

So shepherds were squinting and blinking, and shepherds began to listen, but none of them had the courage to talk or to answer a thing.

"For unto you is born this day in the city of David," said the angel, "a Savior, who is Christ the Lord. And this will be a sign for you: you will find the babe wrapped in swaddling clothes and lying in a manger."

Suddenly, the sky itself split open, and like the fall of a thousand stars, the light poured down. There came with the angel a multitude of the heavenly host, praising God and saying.

"Glory to God in the highest,
And on earth, peace—
Peace to the people with whom he is pleased!"

But hush, you shepherds. Hush in your wonder. For the choral singing soon was ended. The hosts ascended, and the sky was closed again. And then there came a breeze and a marvelous quiet and the simple dark of the night. It was just that, no terror in that then. It was only the night, no deeper gloom than evening. For not all of the light had gone back into heaven. The Light of the World himself stayed down on earth and near you now.

And you can talk now. Try your voices. Try to speak. Ah, God has given you generous voices, shepherds. Speak.

So then, this is what the shepherds said to one another:

"Let us," they said, "go to Bethlehem and see this thing that has happened, which the Lord has made known to us."

So the shepherds got up and ran as fast as they could to the city of Bethlehem, to a particular stable in that city, and in that stable they gazed on one particular baby, lying in a manger.

Then, in that moment, everything was fixed in a lambent, memorial light.

For there was the infant, just waking, just lifting his arms to the air and making sucking motions with his mouth. The holy child was hungry. And there was his mother, lying on straw as lovely as the lily and listening to the noises of her child. "Joseph?" she murmured. And there was Joseph, as sturdy as a barn, just bending toward his Mary. "What?" he whispered.

And the shepherds' eyes were shining for what they saw.

Exactly as though it were morning and not the night, the shepherds went out into the city and began immediately to tell everyone what the angel had said about this child. They left a trail of startled people behind them, as on they went, both glorifying and praising God.

But Mary did not so much as rise that night. She received the baby from Joseph's hands, then placed him down at her breast while she lay on her side on straw. With one arm she cradled the infant against her body. On the other arm, bent at the elbow, she rested her head; and she gazed at her small son sucking. Mary lowered her long, black lashes and watched him and loved him and murmured, "Jesus, Jesus" for the baby's name was Jesus.

"Joseph?" she said without glancing up.

And Joseph said, "What?"

But Mary fell silent and said no more. She was keeping all these things—all that had happened between the darkness and the light—and pondering them in her heart.

Christmas Prayer

John Leax

Let the snow fall this night
and cover our sins
against the world

Let the scars of our restless flight
from nothing to nowhere
be iced and closed

Let the wires of our false security
be weighted to breaking
and the lamps of our burning earth
be darkened

Let nothing remain
in the emptiness of our hearts
but the dark of need

In that dark
let one star shine

And grant us grace to spring
in the quickening light
it angles at creation

Star Song

Luci Shaw

We have been having
epiphanies, like suns,
all this year long.
And now, at its close
when the planets
are shining through frost,
light runs
like music in the bones,
and the heart keeps rising
at the sound of any song.
An old magic flows
in the silver calling
of a bell,
rounding
high and clear,
flying, falling,
sounding
the death knell
of our old year,
the new appearing
of Christ, our Morning Star.

Now burst!
all our bell throats.
Toll!
every clapper tongue.
Stun the still night!

Jesus himself gleams through
our high heart notes
(it is no fable).
It is he whose light
glistens in each song sung
and in the true
coming together again
to the stable,
of all of us: shepherds,
sages, his women and men,
common and faithful,
wealthy and wise,
with carillon hearts
and, suddenly,
stars in our eyes.

Letter to Friends – Advent, 1990

John Leax

Twice snow has fallen
and stilled the chirring squirrel.
Its increase will end
the song Salvation Brook
sings trickling to the river.

But not yet.

The sun has life enough
to reach the trees.

Soon I will close myself
behind the cabin door
and spider my words
across the page
in propane warmth.

But not yet.

The fire between my shelter
and the chilling wind prevails.

What loneliness that drives
me out from you
to wait in emptiness as cold
slowly claims the land
will be assuaged.

But not yet.

The time of cold is not
the time to turn aside.

The dark will descend.
The wood will be held
in the lock of ice,
and the Word, quiet
as a star, will come.

But not yet.

These words are my words.
Wait. Wait.

Chance

Luci Shaw

Did God take his chances
on a son sent to fill flesh?
Was such metamorphosis
a divine risk?

Once embodied
might he not find
earth's poignancies too sharp,
sweet flesh too sweet
to soon discard?
Might not man's joys
  (the growing
  of body, mind, and will,
  knowing
  companionship,
  the taste of shared bread,
  the smell of olives
  new-carved wood, and wine,
  morning's chill
  on a bare head,
  rough warm wool,
  a near, dust-blue Judean hill,
  evening's shine
  of oil lamps through an
  open door,
  day's work, tired muscles
  a bed on the floor)

make up for his limitations?
Might he not even
wish for a peaceful death
from old age?

Ah, Father, but you knew
the incarnation was no gamble!
We are the risk you run.

Across the purple-patterned snow

Luci Shaw

Across the purple-patterned snow
laced with light of lantern-glow,
dappled with dark,
comes Christ, the Child born
    from the skies.
Those are stars that are his eyes.
His baby face is wise
seen by my candle spark.
But is he cold from the wind's
    cold blow?
Where will he go?

I'll wrap him warm with love,
well as I'm able,
in my heart stable!

The Adoration of The Magi

Madeleine L'Engle

Very different from the simple shepherds were the wise men who came from three different parts of the globe, a long journey that must have taken them well over a year. They were serious scholars who studied the heavens and the movement of the heavenly bodies. They were both astronomers and astrologers, and we have not seen their like since astronomy and astrology were separated many centuries ago.

The wise men were wise men indeed, men of great intellectual sophistication; but each one saw the birth of an unknown child as an event of unprecedented proportion and each one left home to make the long trip to Judea because of what he had read in the movement of the planets and the stars. They understood that the birth of a single child could affect the entire universe, just as physicists today understand that all of creation is a single organism. Nothing happens in isolation. The crying of a baby sends sound waves to galaxies thousands of light years away.

So these ancient astronomers believed that something was happening in Bethlehem that would change the world. They met on the way, going first to Jerusalem and speaking to Herod, the king of Judea. "Where is the child who has been born the King of the Jews? We have seen his sign in the East and have come to worship him."

Herod knew nothing of the new king, and he tried to hide his immediate and frantic jealousy of a baby who might grow up to take over his throne. He sent the wise men on to Bethlehem, not far from Jerusalem, saying, "Go and search diligently for the child; and when you have found him, come and tell me, that I may worship him also."

The wise men went to Bethlehem and found Mary, Joseph and the child. Bethlehem was a little town, so they would have had no difficulty asking directions; and all eyes would have been drawn to them in their exotic garments, riding on magnificent horses, with a retinue of servants, and camels and other beasts.

The child himself was too young to be astonished, but Mary and Joseph were awed by the splendid visitation. First the simple shepherds and now these noble wise men. But what could be too great for a child born of Heaven, a child who would always carry a double nature, that of God and that of man.

The wonder of the Incarnation can only be accepted with awe. Jesus was wholly human, and Jesus was wholly divine. This is something that has baffled philosophers and theologians for two thousand years. Like love, it cannot be explained, it can only be rejoiced in. Did the wise men understand this Glorious Impossible? Perhaps they came close. They left gifts of gold, frankincense, and myrrh; and being warned in a dream not to go back to Herod, they returned to their homes by another way.

A celibate epiphany

Luci Shaw

An apple is meant to be
flower & food & tree
& if it goes to rot, what
of its destiny?

See,
here is a woman, planned
to be manned:
lover & mother
Single, she
is other
knowing only a kind
of atrophy
(even an apple's designed
to be eaten or climbed)
and who but God
can exorcise
the trauma
of her empty thighs?
Between his palms' dance
he twirls her brittle stem.
His fingers
touch her virgin hem.
His light shines,
lingers,
& all glories glance
upon her inward parts.

His purpose finds
her heart of hearts,
conceiving Jesus
at her core
by his most
Holy Ghost. Once more,
as with lonely Mary, he
makes of her,
in her own time
& in his time, his sweet
bride, also a tree
thick enough to climb
with petals
for the eye's delight
& fruit to eat.

Vigil: Christmas Eve, 1991

John Leax

From this dark wood, dormant
in star shine,
the squirrels still in the bounty
of oak abundance,
the mice curled close beneath
the insulating snow,
nothing is far.

Here, above the valley,
in body numbing cold I wait
to open what descends.
Nothing breaks over me.
Night is all. It holds me,
and lost in the loss
of sense, I ask nothing.

From the houses below
where friends dwell in peace
lights as steady as stars
rise to greet my watch.
No angel will descend.
All there is to see I see:
Christ is in His world.

Small Gifts

Karen Burton Mains

One morning, with a writing deadline looming, I rolled out of bed, aimed myself with eyelids at half-mast in the direction of the kitchen coffee pot, toted a steaming mug back upstairs to my study. The urgency of creative commitments pre-empted my morning routine. I didn't bother with makeup, ran a comb hastily through my hair, brushed my teeth, then still wearing the sweatsuit I had slept in, met my grim appointment with my computer, determined to satisfy this editor on time.

While in this dowdy state, looking frumpish and every inch forty-seven, the doorbell rang-at 8 o'clock in the morning. The delivery man from Bob's Salt and Feed had a load of salt for the water softener. I stood in the kitchen, having shoved my bare feet into the too-big pair of grown son's footgear (the only shoes handy when I needed them), and with my checkbook poised in hand as he carried the heavy blocks to the basement for me. "Haven't seen you for a while," he grinned in passing, his voice trailing him down the stairs.

"Nope," I called, wishing I had at least put on some lipstick. My floppy gym shoes were hidden beneath the kitchen stool rungs. I could hear him coming back up the stairs. "Say," he said as he headed out the back door, through the garage, and to his flatbed truck, "Ain't no salt left down there."

"That's why I called you guys," I answered back. I wrote "Bob's Salt and Feed" on check #761. Two more trips down stairs, up the stairs, brought the delivery man finally to my kitchen counter. He was big, middle-aged, bearded and wearing working man's overalls. I felt somehow vulnerable with his presence in my kitchen space and having to deal with him barefaced. Charm, my requisite commodity of tradesmen, deserted me this morning. He handed me a handwritten bill.

"Say. Since the last time I was here," he said as I hurriedly wrote out the check, "I got me a Maine coon kitty."

"A what?"

"A Maine coon kitty. Maine coon cats are the oldest breed there is. The vet told me. That kitty is six months old and he weighs sixteen pounds already. They grow real big. His tail is that round." The delivery man made a circle with both of his large hands to show me.

I handed him the check, then the Bob's Salt and Feed man left, closing the door behind him. The house quieted, and I returned to my computer, but sitting there I realized I was unaccountably warmed by this incident. A lovely gift had been given me. A grown man had been bursting with a boy's good news. Somehow, he had trusted that I would want to hear about his treasure, that I would know what a find a Maine coon kitty was.

And the truth was: I didn't want to hear. Sitting in my study upstairs, I was suddenly delighted by the incongruity of the child-like joy of this middle-aged man. "This big," I kept hearing him saying, seeing his large hands making a circle the size of the kitty's tail. Strangely, that morning which had begun with my determined, grim effort at writing suddenly turned to joy. He got him a Maine coon kitty, I thought. And was glad.

I have a New York City friend who every so often brings me small gifts from Tiffany's. I must confess that there is a part of me given to luxury. I love the neat suede packets that house the jewelry, the little boxes, the egg-shell blue ribbon that hallmarks this jeweler's giftwraps.

But strangely enough, I am moved mostly by other small gifts, the shopping bag full of acorn squash my church secretary brings to me from her garden, " You said you wanted a lot." The phone voice of a mental hospital inmate who has called collect so that he can read his poem to me; "Karen?" he says, sounding gravelly from the drugs. "I wrote a new poem called Snow-mornings. I thought you would like to hear it." A four-year old child who invariably comments on my appearance, "Oh, you look very boo-ti-ful, Karen. You look very boo-ti-ful." (I am beginning to dress for Chelsea's pleasure.) A male acquaintance who likes to plan social events with me, "Weren't we going to hold our First Annual Grand Croquet Match this summer together? How many should we invite? Around a hundred? Shall we have everyone wear white? " My daughter's friend who includes me in the horseback riding plans, "I'm going riding this Sunday. Do you want to come?" The horse which, saddled, rests his nuzzle in the cup of my palms, still for five minutes as we wait for the others; reading me, monitoring what kind of human I am. The smile of the stranger in the airport terminal inviting me to chat while we wait together for our delayed plane. My son-in-law who skates backwards, pulling me with his hands until I finally feel steady on the ice after all these years.

These are the gifts that warm me, make me feel wanted, show me that in the meaning of another's life I have meaning. The well-known Christian leader who phones, "I was thinking of you and just wondered what you are doing." The pastor who says, "Can we have coffee? We haven't had time just to talk." "I had a funny dream about you," reports a younger woman in my life. "I'll tell you what I dreamed and you tell me what it means!"

These small gifts, these almost off-handed, throw-away spontaneous things are what fill me with a mighty joy.

My father-in-law and his male friend, two older men whose wives are both suffering from Alzheimer's Disease, wear suits and ties to the special Sunday evening supper I have planned for them. They linger over the meal and tell old-time stories and we laugh together. They make a big deal over the poached salmon. "Was that broiled or poached?" my father-in-law asks me the next day on the phone. "That fish was so good."

Why is it we think we must be extravagant in our giving? Why is it we go to such great expenses? Or wear ourselves out shopping?

Or perhaps it is only I who is undone by simple gestures, by a man's exultation over a Maine coon kitty.

Yet Scripture often makes note of the simple things: a child's lunch. The widow's mite. The words, "I believe. . ." A baby born in Bethlehem, one baby out of so many. God also seems to delight in taking ordinary circumstances, the normal events of daily living, the small tools in our hands (like the excess garlic bulbs placed into a sack for me by the hostess of a bed and breakfast); and he then turns them into extraordinary occurrences, poignant with meaning. I do not want to overlook the simple gifts, to become so busy I miss seeing their rare beauty. I do not want to miss this God-like propensity to wonder at the common.

Christmas should be a time of simple givings. Advent is a matter of looking for Christ-comings, of getting ready to mark nativity as it peeks through in small ways today, and today. And today. And today. Christ is amassed all the year in these epiphanies, in these common showings made uncommon, in the power of the everyday unmasked.

So bring me the simple gifts if you love me. And God, give me grace to see them.

Our Lady of I-80

Calvin Miller

On our 30th wedding anniversary, I took my wife's old engagement ring to a jeweler and had him lift the diamond from its modest mounting and set it down in a new cluster of outrageous sparkle. The result was exquisite.

After 30 years, that diamond, although something of great value, had quit speaking—precisely because it had spoken for so long in the same way. Now its new enhancement caused it to proclaim the older covenants with a glistening new vigor. Something old and precious received new voice by being set in a newer context.

A similar recasting is often necessary at Christmas. Familiarity breeds a dull Noel. Because there are only a few Scripture passages that describe the Christmas story, each December we may hear all of them four and five times. We enter Yuletide with yawns, perhaps even envying the shepherds who heard the first rendition of "Peace on earth." What woke them in joy, puts us to sleep!

We find ourselves in love with the season, but dulled by its ever-cycling familiarity. If the story is so wonderful, why so often doesn't it seem that way?

A few years ago, a sharply dressed business man from our church was crossing our state on Inter-state 80, that 450-mile stretch of highway that bisects Nebraska from west to east. Somewhere west of Omaha, he passed a couple hitchhiking. They were obviously poor. The woman looked very cold—and very pregnant.

My friend picked them up and brought them to Omaha. With the help of others, he arranged for their housing. About a month later, the child was born.

Just before the baby's birth, I was invited to a dinner at an elegant home in honor of the rescued couple. They were rustic and a bit uncouth. The woman, now great with child, often belched embarrassingly loudly during the festive affair. The upper-middle-class guests looked greatly chagrined.

I must confess that I, too, felt an unspoken sternness as I beheld the poor couple. I did not immediately liken them to you know who from Luke 2. But later I did wonder, if I had been running a Holiday Inn in Bethlehem, whether I would have asked them to please stay at the Best Western. . . or offered them the barn out-back. Especially if the woman had told me that their Blue Cross had expired and she was having labor pains!

Every time I now hear the Christmas story, I think about this couple. I don't like the similarities I see between myself and the inn-keeper in Bethlehem that first century night when a couple of hitchhikers were in trouble. But I do know that the Christmas story will never be quite the same for me again.

A Victorian Plum Pudding

Barbara Miller

*Hallo! a great deal of steam! The pudding was out of the
copper. A smell like a washing day! That was the cloth. A smell like
an eating house and a pastry-cook's next door to each other, with a
laundress's next door to that! That was the pudding . . . like a
speckled cannon-ball, so hard and firm, blazing in half of half a
quarter of ignited brandy, and bedlight with Christmas Holly
stuck to the top.*
—Charles Dickens, *A Christmas Carol*

4 slices of bread torn in pieces
1 cup milk
2 cups beef suet, ground
8 ounces of brown sugar
2 slightly beaten eggs
1/4 cup orange juice
1 teaspoon vanilla
1 1/2 cups raisins
3/4 cup snipped dates
1/2 cup diced mixed candied fruit and peel
1/2 cup chopped walnuts
1 cup flour
1 teaspoon baking soda
1/2 teaspoon salt
2 teaspoons cinnamon
1 teaspoon cloves
1 teaspoon mace

Soak bread pieces in the milk. Stir in the suet, sugar, eggs, orange juice and vanilla. Mix together the raisins, dates, fruit and walnuts. Mix together the flour, soda, salt, cinnamon, cloves and mace. Add the flour mixture to the fruit mixture and then stir into the suet mixture. Pour into a greased pudding mold. Steam for 3 ¹/₂ hours. Cool at least 10 minutes before unmolding. Cut pudding and serve with Hard Sauce.

Hard Sauce

Cream together 1/2 cup butter and 1 teaspoon vanilla. Add 2 cups sifted powdered sugar and cream until fluffy. Beat in 1 egg yolk and then stir in 1 stiff, beaten egg white.

Wassail Bowl

Barbara Miller

Wassail, wassail all over the town!
Our bread it is white and our ale is brown;
Our bowl is made of the maple tree,
So here, my good fellow, I'll drink to thee.

The wass'ling bowl with a toast within,
Come, fill it up now unto the brim.
Come fill it up that we may all see,
With the wassailing bowl, I'll drink to thee.
—Traditional English Carol

2 quarts apple cider
1 - 1/2 cups sugar
2 teaspoons whole allspice
2 teaspoons whole cloves
5 cinnamon sticks
4 cups cranberry juice
2 cups orange juice
1 cup lemon juice

Combine cider and sugar in large pan. Tie cloves, allspice, and cinnamon sticks in a cloth bag or other porous container; add to the cider mixture, cover and simmer 20 minutes. Remove the spice bag and discard. Add the remaining ingredients and simmer 15 minutes. Garnish with orange and lemon slices. Serve hot. Makes about 1 gallon.

The Secret Stair

Shirley Nelson

The MacDonalds had been living in the big old farmhouse down the road from us for only six months when Mrs. MacDonald ran away. That was in the summer of 1934. In the course of the next winter, four other women came to take care of the two boys—a grandmother, an aunt, a hired housekeeper, and another younger woman whose role was uncertain. None of them stayed.

The boys, Bart and Luke, were eight and ten. My sisters and I sometimes played with them in the fields between our houses, though we didn't really like them. We thought they were strange. They called their parents Marcia and Mac instead of Mom and Dad, and ate candy in front of us between meals. Bart, the younger, was a cry-baby and ran home at the slightest offence.

After their mother went away, they never talked about her, and we never asked, since our parents had ordered us not to. Then that Easter of 1935, the boys suddenly appeared at our back door in the middle of the afternoon, all dressed up in suits and red bow ties. "We can't play with you today," announced Luke. "We have to stay clean."

"Because Marcia is coming to visit," said Bart, "and she won't be back til Christmas."

Then he went crazy in a show-off sort of way, running around in a little circle and imitating a monkey. They both seemed excited, but not really glad. In a moment they tore off toward home, punching and kicking each other all the way across the fields. Early in the following October, the unthinkable happened. Our family moved in with the MacDonalds. I mean, we moved out of our own house altogether and into theirs, we three girls with our parents, in with the two MacDonald boys and their father. I thought my parents had lost their senses.

Here is how it happened. One Sunday in September, Mr. MacDonald, a man taller and stronger than our father, stunned us by bursting into tears in our front parlour. His boys had no mother, he sobbed. He had been forced to divorce her on the grounds of desertion. He had tried to get housekeepers, but none would stay. They all hated that old-fashioned kitchen. He had just gotten new work on the railroad and would have to be gone from home for days at a time. Wouldn't we come and live in his big nine-room house, make the boys part of our family, just for the winter?

There he sat in his ankle-high black boots, steel-toed (Bart had told me so), choking and wiping his eyes with his hands like a little boy. He would continue to pay the rent, he said, if my father would buy the food. That would help us a little bit, too, wouldn't it? He had heard we were up against it as well.

It was no secret that we were behind in our own rent. My father worked as a clerk in the grocery store down town, and his salary had been cut twice in the past year. My parents looked at each other across the room and passed a silent yes between them. I knew it would never work, but I was only nine and not asked for my opinion.

I had a hunch my parents were doing it more to help those boys than to help themselves. What they seemed to be disregarding was that the MacDonalds were not like any family we had ever met in our Massachusetts town. They were particularly not like us. Their names alone were exotic. Our name was Brown, and our first names suitably ordinary: I was Annie, my sisters Joan and Peggy, my parents Robert and Mary—whom we called, like normal children, Daddy and Mom. At our house we ate three meals a day, went to bed at the same time each night (with proper resistance), attended school when we were supposed to and did our chores. The MacDonalds seemed to have no rules at all. The boys played hookie when they felt like it, and they went to the movies at least once a week, even at night.

Even before Mrs. MacDonald ran away, I knew she was not a regular mother. On the one occasion when I had entered their house with Bart, she was lying on the couch in the parlour, reading a book, still in her bathrobe, though it was 4:00 in the afternoon. Then, instead of just saying, "Oh, hello, Annie," as other mothers I knew would do, she sat up, put down her book, and wrapped me in a big hug. "Well, hey there, sugar," she said in my ear. "What can I get you? Would you like an orange?"

That was how I saw the inside of their icebox. It was a dismal sight. There was nothing in it except a few oranges, a bottle of ketchup with black gummy stuff around the cap. Our icebox at home, even when money was scarce, always contained real food—part of an apple pie, the ends of cold-cuts my and bowls of left-overs covered with wax paper and elastic bands. Mrs. MacDonald obviously never cooked.

But admittedly, she was beautiful—or rather, I thought, handsome, in the same blond and angular way Mr. MacDonald was handsome. Her nose was straight and masculine, duplicated exactly on her son Bart. Luke had his father's nose, with a full downward curve. Even their noses set them apart from us. Ours were rather short, round-nostriled affairs. In fact, I had always thought of our family as undistinguished in our looks, with our freckles and plain brown hair. Bart and Luke were young gods by comparison, and spoiled ones besides.

That winter was full of surprises. First of all, the nine rooms turned out to be only four. Half of the house was useless, because the coal furnace was out of commission. The upper bedrooms over the closed-off double parlour were too cold even for sleeping. We all lived in the back of the house, in the big kitchen, warmed by a wood-burning range, and in what had once been a dining room, where a kerosene stove connected to the chimney in the fireplace. We dressed and undressed around the two stoves (boys in the dining room, girls in the kitchen), washing and brushing our teeth in the pantry sink (an iron pump there our only source of water), and combing our hair in front of a mirror in a kitchen corner. At night we hurried up the kitchen stairs to our bedrooms and crawled between blankets warmed by hot-water bottles and soap stones.

It was crowded. We had sold our furniture to pay the back rent and it was a good thing. The farmhouse apparently came "as is," including massive pieces of Victorian furniture in every room. There among the tall highboys and platform rockers, the MacDonalds had inserted their modern square plush chairs, a chromy kitchen table, and floor-standing ash trays so big they seemed like pieces of furniture in themselves.

In these jam-packed quarters we managed to co-exist, though we scrapped with the boys almost constantly. Mr. MacDonald was gone most of the time. In a way that made things easier. My family could institute its own agenda. Or try. Bart resisted any kind of structure, but Luke seemed to like it. He especially enjoyed my mother's meals. "You are a good cook, Mrs. Brown," he said expansively one night at supper, which made my sisters and me giggle with embarrassment. We *might* say the pie was good, or the doughnuts, but we never said, "Mother, *you* are a good cook."

Bart, on the other hand, consistently left food on his plate. At times I saw him deliberately drop food on the floor, as if by accident. Once I saw him sneak a handful of cooked carrots into the pocket of his knickers. After the evening meal, it was the children's job to clean up the kitchen. There were lots of dishes. We did them in the cold pantry, the water heated on the stove. Every dish had to be dried and put away. Someone had to wipe off the table and sweep the floor. The boys were no good at this. Bart always pretended to go to the bathroom right after the meal. He put on his jacket and sat out in the cold shed privy until the work was done. If Luke went out to get him they had fist fights, which my mother could not stand, and when my father went to get him Bart pleaded constipation. My father was a gentle man, not one to yank a boy off the toilet.

One Saturday early in November, Mr. MacDonald pulled into the driveway in his old Dodge. It was the first we'd seen of him since we moved in. "Mac! Mac!" the boys screamed. The three greeted each other with a great profusion of shouts and long tender embraces. For half an hour he sat with them on his lap, though they were much too big for that, exchanging news and whispering and laughing. And the next thing we knew he was beating them out in the shed.

I stood with Peggy and Joan in the dining room where our mother sent us, our hands over our ears, eyes wide with horror at the howls and cries and the sucking thwacks of the leather belt. We were never spanked ourselves. We had never felt an angry hand on our bottoms or a switch across the legs. If we were naughty we were made to sit on chairs until we "thought we could behave."

My father was at work or he might have been able to intervene. Mr. MacDonald, sitting at the kitchen table with the boys, had asked my mother how things were going. She said fine, except that—and this in a teasing manner—they were shirking their chores. Then Joan, who was too young to be careful, said, "Yeah! Bart goes to the bathroom when it's time to dry!"

"Mrs. Brown," said Mr. MacDonald, his face suddenly red, "my boys are not to give you the slightest bit of trouble. That was a bargain. *Are* they any trouble to you?"

"Trouble?" asked my mother. "Oh, well, of course they are a *little* trouble."

All she meant, I knew, was the trouble of feeding them, putting up their lunches, washing and mending their clothes, refereeing their fights. She went on to explain, but Mr. MacDonald cut her off.

"Boys!" he barked, tumbling them off his lap. "You were not to give Mrs. Brown any trouble! Out to the shed!"

Even then, we girls had no idea what was about to happen. Bart ran to hide upstairs. My mother protested, but it made no difference. Luke was first, then Bart, dragged out from under a bed. In my mind I leaped into the picture throwing myself against the father, biting and scratching and snatching the belt from his hands—to save these two boys I had often felt like hitting myself.

"It's none of our business," said my mother, firmly. "We have no right to interfere."

Then it was over, as if nothing had happened. The boys washed their faces and Mr. MacDonald bundled us all into his car and drove us to Framingham for ice cream cones. You must understand that to get into a car for the specific and only purpose of going after ice cream in the middle of a day was unheard of in our family.

All the way there Mr. MacDonald recited "Little Annie Rooney," and all the way back he sang sad Scotch ditties, with tears running down his cheeks. Back home he turned on the radio and grabbed my mother's hand and whirling her around the kitchen floor, until her face was red from laughter. I had never seen my mother look like that. Then he stood us one by one on top of his steel-toed shoes and taught us the steps. The next morning he served my parents pancakes in bed, which made them feel foolish. He washed all the dishes, cracking the glasses with boiling water, and washed the kitchen floor. That afternoon we pulled molasses taffy, sticking up the floor he had just washed. After supper he searched through a box of books and gathered the five of us around him on the couch while he read a story so thrilling it took my breath away—*At the Back of the North Wind*, written by (as he told us) "another MacDonald, a very wonderful MacDonald," the author of many stories and poems. He read throughout the entire evening, and we were allowed to stay up past our bedtime to the end of the book.

On Monday morning he was gone again. Bart and Luke produced the dollar bills he had given them in the shed, and Bart pulled up his pajama shirt, all proud smiles, to show me the marks on his back. "It didn't hurt a bit," he boasted.

Other than a few postal cards, we heard nothing more from Mac (as we all now called him) until the day before Christmas. We were trimming the tree after supper and chores when he burst through the kitchen door, wearing a Santa hat and hauling a huge sack of presents. He heaped them around the tree, a shameless excess of bulky white shapes, not just for the boys but for all of us.

"And now," he said, as he straightened up, "it's time to go caroling. On Beacon Hill."

"Beacon Hill?" said my father. "But that's in Boston."

"Certainly. Have you and your girls ever been caroling on Beacon Hill?" Of course we hadn't. Then we must, Mac insisted. We must have that experience. "It's sheer enchantment", he said. "Elegant houses standing right on the sidewalk, decorations from Europe in the windows. Everybody goes caroling on Beacon Hill on Christmas Eve. The MacDonalds are going and we invite the Browns."

It took my parents a long time to make up their minds. There was too much to do, it was an hour away, it was too cold. Finally, what must have been at great cost to their better judgment, they said we girls could go but they themselves would stay home to get ready for tomorrow. I was terribly excited. We had never been to Boston.

Like everything Mac initiated, the excursion was a distinct mixture of pleasure and confusion. It was indeed bitterly cold, and we girls were too short to see into many of the windows. But I was thrilled by the city and loved the dignified houses on the hill, the sense of being part of a crowd, the little clusters of carolers with their voices colliding and mingling up and down the block. We made our own choir of boy and girl sopranos, Mac directing us with flourish, while people listened at their doors and applauded.

Mac was beside himself. He wanted us to see everything and lifted us one by one up to the best windows, with an elaborate running commentary on the scenes laid out of the sills. When it was my turn to look at a particular creche, he exclaimed in my ear, "There it is! There it is!"

"You mean the baby," I said. A baby was all I could see. The entire display consisted of an exquisite life-size china doll lying in straw, holding his toes and laughing.

"That's the secret stair," said Mac. Stair? I saw no stair.

"'They all were looking for a king . . . to slay their foes and lift them high!' said Mac, dramatically, in his poetry-reciting voice. "Thou cam'st a little baby thing' . . . Oh, dear. I've forgotten it."

"Stair?" I asked, completely baffled.

"'Thou com'st down thine own secret stair,' "Mac went on, reciting again. 'Com'st down to answer all my need' . . . I think that's how it goes."

I glanced into the room behind the baby, still looking for a stair. None was in sight. A family sat around a table, drinking something from steaming cups. Cocoa, I thought. A deep hunger and thirst seemed to rise right out of my toes. I wanted that cocoa, that warm bright house, and something else I could feel but not name.

"That's George MacDonald," said Mac.

"Where?" I asked. But he didn't answer. He set me down. It

was Peggy's turn to see.

We arrived home chilled through and cranky with weariness. Bart and I were fighting as we entered the house. We were mortified to discover that we had fallen asleep next to each other in the car.

By noon the next day, Mac had taken off once more. Marcia was coming at 2:00. All this time the boys had not spoken of their mother, except once when Luke stopped in the middle of a game and announced, "Sometimes I miss my mother so much I get a funny taste in my mouth." That afternoon I got my second look at Mrs. MacDonald. I know I stared, thinking there might be something in her face that would distinguish her as a mother who ran away. She was as beautiful as ever, and more quiet than I recalled. There were no squeals of greeting from the boys. They were shy in her presence. She teased and cajoled them playfully to get them to come to her, but they wouldn't until she suddenly cried out, "Oh, my boys, my boys!" and Luke ran to her side.

She stayed only two hours and as she left my father threw on his jacket and walked with her out to the car. When he came back he said grimly, "They are not seeing her letters."

"I thought so," said my mother. "Well, that's one we can fix."

I knew mail had come from her regularly to the boys, which my mother had saved unopened and handed over to Mac on his visits, as he had directed. For the rest of the winter, we ran a mail service between the boys and their mother, reading her letters aloud to them and writing back with news.

"Mac will be mad when he finds out," I said one day to my mother.

"Let him," she said. "He has no right to intercept her mail."

"Even if she's a terrible woman?"

"Ah," replied my mother. "Is this what you think? Well, things are not always as they appear."

It was all over in March anyway, when Mac returned one last time to get the boys. He took them to New Jersey, where he had found a new job, a new house, and a new wife. We never saw them again and soon we ourselves moved.

Life was easier without them, and for a long time I was glad they were gone. Yet for years whenever I would read a book, I pictured its events in and around that old farmhouse, with all the characters wearing the faces of the MacDonalds. Then I would miss them in a way I couldn't explain, maybe a little as Luke described missing his mother... like a funny taste in the mouth.

One Night Only
Handel's Messiah

Philip Yancey

Just before Christmas of 1988, my wife and I visited London. As the plane banked sharply over the city's center, we saw rowing crews on the Thames, and also Parliament, Whitehall Palace, and other landmark buildings lit in sepia by the slanting rays of the morning sun. A fingernail moon hung low in the sky, and the morning star still shone. This was one of London's rare, perfect winter days.

Later that day, half-drunk on coffee, we were dragging along city streets, trying to wrench our biological clocks forward seven time zones by staying awake until dusk. Just before turning in, we lined up in a queue to order some theater tickets. That's when I saw the poster: "One Night Only. Handel's *Messiah* performed by the National Westminster Choir and National Chamber Orchestra at the Barbican Centre." The ticket seller assured me that of all *Messiah* performances in London, this was clearly the best. There were only two problems: the concert would begin in one hour, and it was sold out.

Twenty minutes later, following some spirited intramarital negotiations, we were in our hotel room squeezing out yet another round of Visine and dressing for a sold-out concert. This moment of serendipity we would not let pass. "Our presence is divinely ordained," I assured my wife. "We are in Handel's home town, where he wrote the piece." Surely a trifling matter like a sellout would not deter us from finding a way inside where we would enjoy an unsurpassed musical experience. Janet's arched eyebrow conveyed unmistakably what she thought of my circumstantial theology, but she indulged me.

After a pell-mell taxi ride to the concert hall, we stumbled across a civic-minded English chap who offered us his extra tickets at half price. My theology was looking better all the time. I started to relax, anticipating a soothing evening of baroque music. Seated on the back row of the main floor, we were ideally positioned for a catnap should the need arise.

I hardly anticipated what I got that evening. I had, of course, heard Handel's *Messiah* often. But something about this time—my sleep-starved, caffeine-buzzed state, the London setting, the performance itself—transported me back closer, much closer, to Handel's day. The event became not just a performance, but a kind of epiphany, a striking revelation of Christian theology. I felt able to see beyond the music to the soul of the piece...

At the London premiere of *Messiah*, King George I had stood for the singing of the "Hallelujah!" chorus. Some skeptics suggest that the king stood to his feet less out of respect for "Hallelujah!" than out of the mistaken assumption that *Messiah* had reached its conclusion. Even today novices in the audience make the same mistake. Who can blame them? After two hours of performance, the music seems to culminate in the rousing chorus. What more is needed?

I had never really considered the question until that night at the Barbican Centre. But as I glanced at the few paragraphs of libretto remaining, I realized what was missing from Parts 1 and 2. They supply the narrative of Jesus' life, but not the underlying meaning. Part 3 steps out from the story and, gathering quotations from Romans, 1 Corinthians, and Revelation, provides that essential layer of interpretation.

In a brilliant stroke, Part 3 of *Messiah* opens with a quotation from Job, that tragic figure who clung stubbornly to faith amid circumstances that called for bleak despair. "I know that my Redeemer liveth, and that he shall stand at the latter day upon the earth," the soprano sings out. Overwhelmed by tragedy, with scant evidence of a sovereign God, Job still managed to believe; and, Handel implies, so should we.

From that defiant opening, Part 3 shifts to the apostle Paul's theological explanation of Christ's death ("Since by man came death . . .") and then moves quickly to his lofty words about a final resurrection ("The trumpet shall sound, and the dead shall be raised").

Just as the tragedy of Good Friday was transformed into the triumph of Easter Sunday, one day all war, all violence, all injustice, all sadness will likewise be transformed. Then and only then we will be able to say, "O death, where is thy sting? O grave, where is thy victory?" The soprano carries that thought forward to its logical conclusion, quoting from Romans 8: "If God be for us, who can be against us?" If we believe, truly believe, that the last enemy has been destroyed, then we indeed have nothing to fear. At long last, death is swallowed up in victory.

Handel's masterwork ends with a single scene frozen in time. To make his point about the Christ of eternity, librettist

Jennens could have settled on the scene from Revelation 2, where Jesus appears with a face like the shining sun and eyes like blazing fire. Instead, his text concludes with the scene from Revelation 4-5, perhaps the most vivid image in the book.

Twenty-four impressive rulers are gathered together, along with four living creatures who represent strength and wisdom and majesty—the best in all creation. These creatures and rulers kneel respectfully before a throne luminous with lightning and encircled by a rainbow. An angel asks who is worthy to break a seal that will open up the scroll of history. Neither the creatures nor the twenty-four rulers are worthy. The author realizes well the significance of that moment, "I wept and wept because no one was found who was worthy to open the scroll or look inside."

Besides these creatures, impotent for the grand task, one more creature stands before the throne. Though appearance offers little to recommend him, he is nevertheless history's sole remaining hope. "Then I saw a Lamb, looking as if it had been slain." A lamb! A helpless, baa-baa lamb, and a slaughtered one at that! Yet John in Revelation, and Handel, sum up all history in this one mysterious image. The great God who became a baby, who became a lamb, who became a sacrifice—this God, who bore our stripes and died our death, this one alone is worthy. That is where Handel leaves us, with the chorus "Worthy Is the Lamb," followed by exultant amens.

We were sitting in a modern brick-and-oak auditorium in the late twentieth century in a materialistic culture light years removed from the imagery of slaughtered lambs. But Handel understood that history and civilization are not what they appear. Auditoriums, dynasties, civilizations—all rise and fall. History has proven beyond doubt that nothing fashioned by the hand of humanity will last. We need something greater than history, something outside history. We need a Lamb slain before the foundations of the world.

I confess that belief in an invisible world, a world beyond this one, does not come easily for me. Like many moderns, I sometimes wonder if reality ends with the material world around us, if life ends at death, if history ends with annihilation or solar exhaustion. But that evening I had no such doubts. Jet lag and fatigue had produced in me something akin to an out-of-body state, and for that moment the grand tapestry woven by Handel's music seemed more real by far than my everyday world. I felt I had a glimpse of the grand sweep of history. And all of it centered in the Messiah who came on a rescue mission, who died and who wrought from that death the salvation of the world. I left with renewed belief that he (and we) shall indeed reign forever and ever.

The Twelve Days of Christmas

Eugene H. Peterson

Day I: The Tree

There shall come forth a shoot from the stump of Jesse, and
a branch shall grow out of his roots.

Isaiah 11:1

Jesse's roots, composted with carcasses
Of dove and lamb, parchments of ox and goat,
Centuries of dried up prayers and bloody
Sacrifice, now bear me gospel fruit.

> *David's branch, fed on kosher soil,*
> *Blossoms a messianic flower, and then*
> *Ripens into a kingdom crop, conserving*
> *The fragrance and warmth of spring for winter use.*

Holy Spirit, shake our family tree;
Release your ripened fruit to our outstretched arms.

> *I'd like to see my children sink their teeth*
> *Into promised land pomegranates*

And Canaan grapes, bushel gifts of God,
While I skip a grace rope to a Christ tune.

Day II: The Star

I see him, but not now; I behold him, but not nigh: a star shall come forth out of Jacob.

Numbers 24:17

No star is visible except at night,
Until the sun goes down, no accurate north.
Day's brightness hides what darkness shows to sight,
The hour I go to sleep the bear strides forth.

    I open my eyes to the cursed but requisite dark,
    The black sink that drains my cistern dry,
    And see, not nigh, not now, the heavenly mark
    Exploding in the quasar-messaged sky.

Out of the dark, behind my back, a sun
Launched light-years ago, completes its run;

    The undeciphered skies of myth and story
    Now narrate the cadenced runes of glory.

Lost pilots wait for night to plot their flight,
Just so diurnal pilgrims praise the midnight.

Day III: The Candle

The people who walked in darkness have seen a great light:
Those who dwelt in a land of deep darkness, on them has
light shined.

Isaiah 9:2

Uncandled menorahs and oilless lamps abandoned
By foolish virgins too much in a hurry to wait
And tend the light are clues to the failed watch,
The missed arrival, the midnight might-have-been.

Wick and beeswax make guttering protest,
Fragile, defiant flame against demonic
Terrors that gust, invisible and nameless,
Out of galactic ungodded emptiness.

Then deep in the blackness fires nursed by wise
Believers surprise with shining all groping derelicts

Bruised and stumbling in a world benighted.
The sudden blazing backlights each head with a nimbus.

Shafts of storm-filtered sun search and destroy
The Stygian desolation: I see. I see.

Day IV: The Time

When the time had fully come, God sent forth his Son, born
of a woman, born under the law, to redeem those who were
under the law, so that we might receive adoption...

Galatians 4:4-5

Half, or more than half, my life is spent
In waiting: waiting for the day to come
When dawn spills laughter's animated sun
Across the rim of God into my tent.

    In my other clock sin I put off
    Until I'm ready, which I never seem
    To be, the seized day, the kingdom dream
    Come true. My head has been too long in the trough.

Keeping a steady messianic rhythm,
Ocean tides and woman's blood fathom

    The deep that calls to deep, and bring to birth
    The seeded years, and grace this wintered earth

Measured by the metronomic moon.
Nothing keeps time better than a womb.

Day V: The Dream

…an angel of the Lord appeared to him in a dream.
Matthew 1:20

Amiably conversant with virtue and evil,
The righteousness of Joseph and wickedness
Of Herod, I'm ever and always a stranger to grace.
I need this annual angel visitation

> *—sudden dive by dream to reality—*
> *To know the virgin conceives and God is with us.*
> *The dream powers its way through winter weather*
> *and gives me vision to see the Jesus gift.*

Light from the dream lasts a year. Impervious
To equinox and solstice it makes twelve months

> *Of daylight by which I see the creche where my*
> *Redeemer lives. Archetypes of praise take shape*

Deep in my spirit. As autumn wanes I count
The days 'til I will have the dream again.

Day VI: The War

And the dragon stood before the woman who was about to
bear a child, that he might devour her child... Now war
arose in heaven.

Revelation 12:4, 7

This birth's a signal for war. Lovers fight,
Friends fall out. Merry toasts from flagons
Of punch are swallowed in the maw of dragons.
Will mother and baby survive this devil night?

 I've done my share of fighting in the traffic:
 Kitchen quarrels, playground fisticuffs:
 Every cherub choir has its share of toughs,
 And then one day I learned the fight was cosmic.

Truce: I lay down arms; my arms fill up
With gifts: wild and tame, real and stuffed

 Lions. Lambs play, oxen low,
 The infant fathers festive force. One crow

Croaks defiance into the shalom whiteness,
Empty, satanic bluster against the brightness.

Day VII: The Carol

Glory to God in the highest, and on earth peace among men with whom he is pleased.

Luke 2:14

Untuned, I'm flat on my feet, sharp with my tongue,
A walking talking discord, out of sorts,
My heart murmurs are entered in lab reports.
The noise between my ears cannot be sung.

    Ill-pleased, I join a line of hard-to-please people
    Who want to exchange their lumpy bourgeois souls
    For a keen Greek mind with a strong Roman nose,
    Then find ourselves, surprised, at the edge of a stable.

Caroling angels and a well-pleased God
Join a choir of cow and sheep and dog

    At this barnyard border between wish and gift.
    I glimpse the just-formed flesh, now mine. They lift

Praise voices and sing twelve tones
Of pleasure into my muscles, into my bones.

Day VIII: The Feast

He who is mighty has done great things for me…He has filled the hungry with good things.

Luke 1:49, 53

The milkful breasts brim blessings and quiet
The child into stillness, past pain: El Shaddai
Has done great things for me. Earth nurses
Heaven on the slopes of the Grand Tetons.

    Grown-up, he gives breakfasts, breaks bread,
    Itinerant host at a million feasts.
    His milkfed bones are buried unbroken
    In the Arimethean's tomb.

The world has worked up an appetite:
And comes on the run to the table he set:
Strong meat, full-bodied wine.

    Wassailing with my friends in the winter
    Mountains, I'm back for seconds as often
    As every week: drink long! drink up!

Day IX: The Dance

When the voice of your greeting came to my ears, the babe
in my womb leaped for joy.

Luke 1:44

Another's heart lays down the beat that puts
Me in motion, in perichoresis, steps
Learned in the womb before the world's foundation.
It never misses a beat: praise pulses.

> *Leaping toward the light, I'm dancing in*
> *The dark, touching now the belly of blessing,*
> *Now the aching side, ready for birth,*
> *For naming and living love's mystery out in the open.*

The nearly dead and the barely alive pick up
The chthonic rhythms in their unused muscles

> *And gaily cartwheel three hallelujahs.*
> *But not all: "Those who are deaf always despise*

Those who dance." That doesn't stop the dance:
All waiting light leap at the voice of greeting.

Day X: The Gift

For to us a child is born, to us a son is given… and his name will be called "Wonderful Counselor, Mighty God, Everlasting Father, Prince of Peace."

Isaiah 9:6

Half-sick with excitement and under garish lights
I do it again, year after year.
I can't wait to plunder the boxes, then show
And tell my friends: Look what I got!

> *I rip the tissues from every gift but find*
> *That all the labels have lied. Stones.*
> *And my heart a stone, "Dead in trespasses*
> *And sin." The lights go out. Later my eyes,*

Accustomed to the dark, see wrapped
In Christ-foil and ribboned in Spirit-colors

> *The multi-named messiah, love labels*
> *On a faith shape, every name a promise*

And every promise a present, made and named
All in the same breath. I accept.

Day XI: The Cradle

And she gave birth to her first born son and wrapped him in
swaddling clothes, and laid him in a manger.

Luke 2:7

For us who have only known approximate fathers
And mothers manque, this child is a surprise:
A sudden coming true of all we hoped
Might happen. Hoarded hopes fed by prophecies,

    Old sermons and song fragments, now cry
    Coo and gurgle in the cradle, a babbling
    Proto-language which as soon as it gets
    A tongue (and we, of course, grow open ears)

Will say the big nouns: joy, glory, peace;
And live the best verbs: love, forgive, save.
Along with the swaddling clothes the words are washed

    Of every soiling sentiment, scrubbed clean of
    All failed promises, then hung in the world's
    Backyard dazzling white, billowing gospel.

Day XII: The Offering

May the kings of Tarshish and of isles render him tribute,
    may the kings of Sheba and Seba bring gifts!
Long may he live,
    may gold of Sheba be given to him!

Psalms 72:10,15

Brought up in a world where there's no free lunch
And trained to use presents for barter, I'm spending
The rest of my life receiving this gift with no
Strings attached, but not doing too well.

    Three bathrobed wise men with six or seven
    Inches of jeans and sneakers showing, kneel,
    Offering gifts that symbolize the gifts
    That none of us is ready yet to give.

A few of us stay behind, blow out the candles,
Sweep up the straw and put the creche in storage.

    We open the door into the world's night
    And find we've played ourselves into a better

Performance. We leave with our left-over change changed
At the offertory into kingdom gold.

Under the Snowing

Luci Shaw

Under the snowing
the leaves lie still.
Brown animals sleep
through the storm, unknowing,
behind the bank
and the frozen hill.
And just as deep
in the coated stream
the slow fish grope
through their own
dark stagnant dream.
Who on earth would hope
for a new beginning
when the crusted snow
and the ice start thinning?
Who would ever know
that the land could stir
with warmth and wakening
coming, creeping,
for sodden root, and fin, and fur
and other things lonely and
cold and sleeping?

Christmas Eve

Robert Siegel

While cattle stupidly stare
over straw damp from their breathing
and the horse lazily stirs
over his trough, and the lantern
licks at shadows in corners,

in the woods the wild ones gather,
the rabbit twitching with care,
sooty shrew, and imperial mole
with the hands of a lost politician,
to shine in the branch-broken light

of a moon which in mid-careen
lights up a church of snow.
Now one paw after another
about the bones of weeds
in a soft worrying circle

the helpless ones dance out their fear,
watching the glittering air
where he shines in the eyes of the others
naked, with nothing to wear.
Long before he comes to the stable

to the shrew's moving smudge on the snow
to the mole's ineffectual gesture
to the soft hide of the hare
he comes, warming each creature
naked in the fangs of the year.

Hopkins, Skipkins & Jumpkins
A Christmas Tale About The Trinity Bunnies

William Griffin

On Christmas Eve in Long Harewood, it was cold and wet to the point of ice.

There were no shepherds abiding in the fields because there were no sheep. No fools they, the woolly creatures stood in their folds, bundling together to keep warm.

And there were no angel voices singing on high. The heavenly choir was at home sick in bed, coughing and spitting and gargling to help their sore throats.

Snow was falling lightly—a dusting of powdered sugar on the branmeal meadows.

It was quiet, ohhh-so-quiet, except for the occasional whistle of a wind through a leafless branch, which, as darkness approached, sounded more like a whine.

Below ground in Long Harewood, however, there was plenty of activity. Invitations had been sent out, and there was a party to go to.

Among the rabbit bucks, the talk was about how difficult it was to get to Burrow Hall. "I hate it when there's no map with the invitation," said one of them, big enough to be a lorry driver.

Among the rabbit does there was a lot of sing-song chatter about how nice it was to dress up and go to a party at this time of year and how easy it would be to get there on the Underground.

"You take the Green Line to Hedgerow, then change to the Red Line for Sheepsbridge, transfer to the Purple Line for Wolfminster, get off at Ramsgate . . ."

As for the rabbit kittens in Long Harewood, they would like the party once they got there, but what they didn't like was being stuffed into stupid sweaters and tight hats with floppy tassels and rubber boots made for giants.

"Welcome to Burrow Hall, welcome," said Hopkins, Skipkins, and Jumpkins to their relatives as they arrived. Stone cold from the trip, they were pointed toward the roaring fireplaces.

"So many new faces since last year," said Skipkins. "Come, take your things off, and warm up with a nice hot cinnamon drink," said Jumpkins.

The guests took off their outer clothes and gave them to Old Harelip, the butler, who trundled them off to a hidden room where he piled them onto a bed. "They'll never find them now," he mumbled.

Once they had warmed themselves, the rabbits moved toward the center of the hall, singing Christmas carols and admiring the little crèche. There the Baby Jesus doll was lying, surrounded by statuettes of three adoring rabbits.

"This looks like the best Christmas Eve party ever," said Hopkins proudly.

"Dinner is served!" shouted Old Harelip in a weak voice, which could barely be heard; then he used a handbell to gather the crowd.

Everyone sat down and grew quiet as Hopkins rose to say the Grace.

"For what we are about to receive this holyday eve, may the Lord make us truly thankful.

"That we rabbits are not what others are about to eat this holiday night," he added, "we are profoundly thankful."

"Amen!" shouted everybody, amused by the little twist of rabbit humor.

There were lots of long tables, each covered with a starched white cloth. Each table had some harebells, blue wildflowers arranged in tiny vases with a little laurel and some red berries.

Each place setting had a china bowl with a Beatrix Potter design. At the left of the plate was a fork; above was a spoon; to the right was a knife. On top of the plate was a folded pink napkin. And there was a Christmas popper.

The first course of the Christmas Eve dinner was the spoon course: all of it had to be eaten with a spoon. Which meant soup. Tureens of hot bubbling soup, guaranteed to burn the tongues of those who slurped too fast.

Parsnip Soup, light yellow at the top, turning to a dark yellow at the bottom, with a deep woodsy taste, served with a dollop of thick white cream.

Onion Soup, a deep brown broth covered with lots of sprinkled cheese that one wanted to dive into to find the onion treasures at the bottom.

Pea Soup, which was a disgusting shade of green, but which, when swallowed on a cold, wet night, became an electric-blanket sort of green, warming one's insides to the point of toast.

"Is it time for the Christmas poppers yet?" purred one little kitten of its mother. "Not yet, dear, not yet."

Between the first and second course of the great dinner, when there was a hush in the hall, Hoppy, the firstborn son of Hopkins, stood up and asked the Question of Questions.

"Why is this night different from all other nights?"

"Because it was on this night two thousand years ago," answered Hopkins, who stood up in full view of the great Burrow Hall, "the first Christmas Eve in Palestine, the night on which the Baby Jesus was born, that we rabbits—the first Hopkins, Skipkins, and Jumpkins—went to the manger to see what the fuss was all about. There we saw the Baby Jesus, and he saw us. We giggled, and he giggled, and I don't suppose I'd be stretching a point if I said that of all the creatures present that holy night so long ago, he liked us rabbits the best. This is why we gather together every year, to remember that special occasion.

The second course of the dinner was the fork course: everything had to be eaten with a fork. No hands allowed.

Chefs came from the kitchen and made the salad, a Cole Slaw, right in front of all the tables.

First, they took white cabbages and red cabbages, green peppers and red peppers, and orange carrots and pushed them back and forth over a sharp blade until the shavings in the huge salad bowl looked like a box of crayons.

Second, they topped the shavings with a milky dressing full of spices.

Third, they tossed the salad high into the air and until it had thoroughly mixed with the dressing.

It was quite a show, clapped the rabbits, but when it came to the eating, not a few in the hall tried to use their hands.

But Old Harelip the butler went about the hall, carrying a

big switch, and twitched the hand of every rabbit—adult or child—who wasn't using a fork.

Between the second and third courses of the great dinner, when there was a hush in the hall, the firstborn son of Skipkins, Skippy, stood up and asked again the Question of Questions.

"Why is this night different from every other night?"

"Because," answered his father, "hundreds of years ago, on Christmas Eve, three rabbits hippity-hopped to Holy Trinity Church, which as you all know is not far from here, to pay their respects to the Baby Jesus. The Vicar surprised them there, but seeing that their ears made a triangle with the Baby Jesus lying in the middle, he was reminded of the Trinity, after which his church was named.

"What did he do after that but paint the scene on a piece of glass, splashing it with a lots of yellow ocher, and had it put into one of the church windows.

"That's why the rabbits in this part of the world visit Holy Trinity Church every Christmas Eve."

The Third and final course of the dinner was baked and could be eaten by hand, but if someone wanted to spread a sweet onto a baked item, then he or she would have to use a knife, or suffer a welt from Old Harelip's switch.

There were Scones and Oatcakes and Hot Cross Buns and Maids of Honor. Onto these the rabbits could lather some Plum Jam or Lemon Curd or Bramble Jelly or Orange Marmalade.

The kittens dove into the desserts and came up with a lot of sticky whiskers. Then they started pulling the strings at the end of the Christmas poppers, filling the hall with the sound of fire-crackers. Old Harelip dove under the nearest table, mumbling, "The hunters are coming! The hunters are coming!"

Antsy for having had to sit so long, the kittens asked when the all-night cartoon festival was going to begin.

"Who's Bugs Bunny?" asked a kitten. "Our American cousin," answered her mother sweetly.

"I didn't get to ask my question," complained Jumpy, the firstborn son of Jumpkins. "I want to ask my question."

"You can ask it," said his father. "I can't ask it now." All the kittens had scampered to the movies. The bucks and does were beginning to move about the dance floor to the delightful music of Happy Hareston and the Hearthmakers. "It's all ruined."

"No, it isn't ruined," said Jumpkins. "I can hear you."

"Why is this night different from every other night?" whispered Jumpy tearily.

"Because we have to go out to find the Baby Jesus tonight and to bring him our presents. And just think. You and Hoppy and Skippy—it will be your turn to go next year."

"But I want to go this year," whined Jumpy.

"Don't be a twit!"

Each carrying a present, Hopkins, Skipkins, and Jumpkins took the Underground to Edgerton, last stop in Long Harewood. Rising to the surface, they could see the steeple of Holy Trinity Church and hear the bell counting ten.

Everything had turned to ice, and everything crinkled under the rabbits' feet. Soon they were separated in the dark, but they all knew where to go.

Suddenly, Hopkins was stopped dead in his tracks by three mean characters: Stoat who carried a machine gun; Ermine who wore high heels and painted her lips red; and Weasel who was a gopher for the gangsters.

"Where do you think you're going, chump?"

"Nowhere!" gulped Hopkins.

"T'anks for my Christmas present!" purred Ermine, as she swiped the square box from Hopkins's hand.

"Seeing as how this is Christmas Eve," grimaced Stoat, "I'm going to let you go."

"Don't look back," hissed Weasel.

Crossing the next field, Skipkins, now separated from his brothers, was set upon by three plump female Owls.

"Who."

"What?" asked Skipkins, knowing that it was difficult to tell just when an Owl was hooting and when it was talking.

"No, I'm Who. She's What," said the first Owl, pointing to the second Owl.

"She's What?" asked Skipkins.

"Yes, she's my sister."

"Ohhh," said Skipkins. "I don't suppose I should ask why."

"You can ask me," said the third Owl whose name was Why, "but I wouldn't waste my time telling a hare-brained creature like you. Give me that present!"

"You can't have it! Give it back! It's for the Baby Jesus!"

"For whom?" asked Who, who took great pride in being grammatically correct.

"The Baby Jesus," shouted Skipkins.

"Forget about it!"

Jumpkins was on the church property now. He should have felt safe, but immediately he felt worse. From the kitchen window of the Vicar's cottage came floating the smell of the evening meal, Saddle of Hare with Onions and Tomatoes. All of a sudden he remembered that the Vicar of Holy Trinity ate nothing but hare and rabbit, which he hunted himself.

Pinching his nose in order not to breathe in the horrid smell, Jumpkins crept toward the church. Suddenly he sneezed and tripped on a hidden wire. It snapped under his foot, sounding like a harp string breaking. Luckily enough, it didn't catch him by the foot or the neck, but it did snatch his Christmas parcel.

At the sound of the sneeze and the twang of the snare, the door to the Vicar's cottage opened, and the holy man appeared with a rifle. "We've got our Christmas dinner," he shouted back to his wife as he came forward in the darkness; "we've got our Christmas dinner!"

The three rabbits, miserable at having lost their presents, met at the little door built hundreds of years ago by their rabbit ancestors, and let themselves inside. The church was cold and dark, but they could see well enough to make their way down the center aisle, where they found the creche.

"What a gyp!" said Jumpkins, looking at the Baby Jesus. "It's just a doll."

"That's funny," said Skipkins; "the baby's eyes are closed. If it were a doll, the eyes'd be open."

"He looks so real," said Hopkins; "I thought I saw him shiver."

"Well, I'm too tired to go back tonight," said Skipkins. "I'm going to sleep in the hay."

They jumped up into the manger. The baby should have felt cold, but instead he felt warm and seemed to be breathing. The rabbits, who were exhausted themselves, cuddled around him, and, as the clock struck midnight, fell into a deep sleep.

I just knew you'd come," said the Baby Jesus, clapping his little hands to wake the rabbits up. The steeple clock was counting three in the morning.

"It *is* you," cried Hopkins. "But a terrible thing's happened.

We've lost all our presents."

"That's all right," said the jolly Baby Jesus. "You're my presents. Let's just do what we do every year?"

What's that?" asked Jumpkins.

"Tell bad rabbit jokes. Who wants to go first?

"Well," said Skipkins, "how many rabbits does it take to change a light bulb?"

"Why does a rabbit wear red suspenders?"

"Why does a rabbit cross the road?"

The worse the joke, the harder they laughed.

"Jokes are the best kind of gift," said the Baby Jesus.

Exhausted from all the laughter, they fell asleep again.

"I thought you didn't bring me any presents," said the Baby Jesus, waking up his friends as the clock struck five.

To the amazement of the rabbits, rubbing the sleepers from their eyes, there on the manger, in the Baby Jesus's lap, were the three packages that had been lost or stolen from them.

"Open mine first," said Hopkins.

The Baby Jesus pulled the paper open and found inside a glass ball. He shook it, and snow began to fall on the Nativity scene inside.

"Open mine next," said Skipkins. Inside his box, resting on a bed of white cotton, was a deep blue bottle; it contained a soapy liquid and a wand with which to blow wobbly bubbles that bounced about and burst.

Jumpkins present was a prism, a piece of cut glass that once hung from a chandelier. Looking through it, the Baby Jesus could see all the pretty colors in the world.

Exhausted, they fell asleep again.

The Vicar turned the big key in the rusty lock and opened

the squeaky church door. Hearing noises, he had come, carrying a pitchfork, to catch the robbers red-handed. Instead, he found, in the crèche at the front of the church, the Baby Jesus asleep with the rabbits around him.

What especially caught the Vicar's eye was that, since there were three rabbits, there should have been six furry ears. But he saw only three, one from each rabbit, forming a sort of triangle around the face of the Baby Jesus.

"Mother, come look at this."

"It's just like the window," she said, looking up to the famous rabbit window, which was hundreds of years old.

"It's my favorite food in the whole world," said the Vicar, backing down the main aisle, "but I don't think I'll ever eat rabbit again."

"And you won't catch me ever again cooking you rabbit either," said the Vicar's wife.

The Holy Child

Christmas, 1840

By Emilie Griffin

She did not find it easy to pray that Christmas, even though the straw in the manger was the same as every Christmas since she had come to the Louisiana village of Grand Coteau. The high voices of the Sisters, singing in Latin and French, those too were the same. Yet in her heart was something—a lump of anguish—that made it hard to pray.

The town was a holy one, founded for the sake of God's work in the Louisiana wilderness, different from the other towns along the bayous of French Louisiana. Everyone knew, Grand Coteau was where the good fathers and the holy sisters lived and taught.

She knelt what seemed forever in the cold chapel and waited for the grace to pray, waited for the angel to swoop down, to cover her with feathers. Under these mighty wings she could trust.

But in the chill, dark pew no angel came; no beating of mighty wings; nothing.

In the chapel of the Sacred Heart were cold kneeling pads. The woman made her devotions every day at the same time according to a prescribed rule. Cornelia Connelly had come so far, though she was a married woman, as to be permitted to pray with the Sisters of the Sacred Heart in the same way and often at the same time. Sometimes, too, she prayed alone in the Chapel of the Sacred Heart, and the angel came down.

What a difference from the last Christmas, 1839. A year ago at Christmas she had first given her heart to the Holy Child.

Then it had been sweet, so sweet: the Holy Child had beamed at her. She had heard the small gurgle of his voice, the high sound of his laughter. She had embraced the third degree of humility, that was part of it all, but so rare for a married woman to do!

That had come a year ago. Such sweetness, such bliss, Cornelia feared she would never know again.

Now there was the darkness, the knife of it, the anger.

She had gained the Holy Child and lost her own child. This was the issue burning between herself and God.

Lord God Almighty, how could you take my John Boy away?

How could you let him fall into the bubbling sugar vat?

How could you let our dear, great Newfoundland dog, lovable-creature, how could you let him, playfully, not understanding, how could you let him nudge my John Boy into the vat?

How was it, Lord, that you did not lift your hand?

How could you not send your legions of angels to catch him as he fell?

How do you expect me to go on believing, now, how do you expect me to forgive?

Is this is the way you treat your friends, Lord?

And why the child?

Why the baby, not me?

I could have taken the burns. I could have taken the hurt. But a two—year—old!

How can you let me, in my mind's eye, see, over and over again, the long hideous moment of his falling, the small self toppling off from the rim of the vat, then splash into the bubbling sugar, and the terrible scream—"Mamma!"

The little voice of the tiny child . . .

Dutch John, his father called him, born overseas, speaking three languages, when he was just one and a half, now gone!

The lilt, the lisp, the little hands clapping, the running, the jumping—all gone.

Child of curls and laughter. Little velvet suits and the precious little starched collar and the wide soft eyes. My son! How could you ask me to forgive it all? Forgive even Sally who let him run too far, up the rim of the vat—but Sally didn't see, she couldn't possibly know—

Look Sally, look how high I can go!

No, John Boy, Sally says no, Mamma says no.

Just to look at the bubbles, Sally, I won't fall,

Just to see.

And the great dog, his protector, the one who always took such good care!

How can I forget!

How can I forgive!

And the forty hours of pain.

Forty, not an hour less, not an hour more, Bible number, like the Lord's forty days, like the Israelites' forty days.

And I wrote in my journal then,

"He was taken up into the temple of the Lord.

This day

On the Feast of the Purification
February second 1840.
I will ask of my Lord without ceasing, and he will give me to
drink."

I wrote that in my journal. I said the perfect things. I wanted
to forgive You perfectly; to make the perfect surrender; to accept, to
relent, to understand.

But I have a knife in my heart, Lord.

Like the sword that pierced your mother's heart, and yes, the
child is with You, You have him. But I kneel here in the chapel,
holding him in my arms, having the smell of him in my nose,
putting my lips deep into his curly head. He is my child, not some
imaginary child, but my flesh, my blood, mine. You have asked too
much, Lord.

Even when You planted another babe in me, you went on tak-
ing away.

St. Edward's Day, we went through the woods, back from Holy
Mass, together, my beautiful husband and I, and he said, inclining
his great intelligent head to mine, he said we would be no more hus-
band and wife. But priest and sister!

And I cried out, I can bear no more of this, I am finished with
pain!

I am unable to offer up my loss
and I wrestled with the angel
on the pathway there
between the convent and the house
where the dirt path winds,
under the oaks,
on the way back to our cottage,
that little house we call Gracemere.

How can I surrender everything to You!
How can I surrender
the times
in that room we call the Bethlehem Chamber,
where my dear husband and I make the little children in the
dark of night?
How can I give that up?
But they are not our children, Lord.
They are yours.
Adeline, and Mercer, and John Boy who is in heaven, and
Mary Magdalene who is in heaven, and the one who is not yet born,
the babe stirring almost I think
they are yours, Lord.
Yours in your holy Childhood.
They are mine because they are Yours.
It is cold here
on the prie dieu
and in the December air of this Louisiana morning
I see my breath dance like frost
and my fingers
clench the prayer book tight,
my fingers turn blue.
And I love you, Holy Child Jesus.
I love you and your Beautiful Mother.
And I bless you for the grace
that brings me to the cradle
in the darkness of your agony and your love.

A Psalm at the Sunrise

Walter Wangerin, Jr.

Omnipotens sempiterne Deus!
Almighty God, the Everlasting, Thou! I cannot look stead-
fastly at the sun and not go blind. Holiness exceeds my sight—
though I know it is, as I know thou art.

Aeterne Deus omnium rerum Creator!
Thou art above all created things. To everything made, thou
art the Other. Greater than thee there is no world; in thee all
worlds have being; and I take my trivial, mortal way upon the
smallest sphere of all. How shall I hope to see thee and not
die?

Lux Mundi!
But in thy mercy thou shinest down upon the things that thou
hast made. They brighten in thy light. Every morning they
reflect thee. I wake to an effulgence of mirrors, and lo: I see.

Misericors Deus!
For my sake, for my poor fleshly sight, thou changest thy
terrible holiness here before me into glory—the visible light,
the doxology I can see. I rise and look around, and I cry praise
to thee.

Deus, incommutabilis virtus, lumen aeternum!
From thee to me it is a mighty diminution: ever the same, thou
makest thy presence manifest in things that are both mutable

and common. But from me to thee it is epiphany: gazing at things most common, suddenly I see thy light, thy glory, and thy face.

Nobiscum Deus!
Then what shall I say to thee but Deo Gratias? Thanks be to God.

Deo gratias!
For the dew that damps the morning grasses is a baptism, always, always renewing the earth. And the air remembers that once it ushered down the dove that was the breath of God. And I myself inhale the rinsed spirit of the morning air and am renewed.

Deo gratias!
For dawn, in the chalices of the clouds, brims them with a bloody wine, a running crimson. And this is a sign to me. The sun is coming.

Deo gratias!
For the sun, when it breaks at the horizon, transfigures every-thing. And this is a gift to me. For the transfiguration itself persuades my soul of sunrise.

Jesu filio Dei gratias!
For I have seen a baby sleeping in a shaft of sunlight, and behold: in the curve of every eyelash was a small sun cupped. From these fringes, tiny rays shot forth to sting me. Sunrise at the far horizon was sunrise near me in this infant.

Et verbum caro factum est—
For the baby suddenly opened her mouth and yawned. And into that pink cavern rushed the sunlight, trembling and flashing like a living thing. But it was thee, bright God, in the mouth of a mortal infant.

"Ecce ego vobiscum sum—"
For the baby woke to the morning and saw me close beside her, and she smiled. Ah, God! What an epiphany of smiling that was! My own transfiguration! For this was the primal light, the glory of the morning, thy splendor and thy face before me come.

Deo gratias, cuius gloria!
Then glory be to thee, Father, Son, and Holy Spirit, as it was in the beginning, is now, and ever shall be, *in saecula saeculorum.*

Amen.

Poems by Calvin Miller

Anthem of the Star

Here is the Festival of Stars!
Now reigns our once and glorious King!
Come and behold Him
Whose splendor is light—
Whose scepter is joyous day—
Whose coming dispels the gathering night—
Whose chariots fly where the bright planets play!
Come children, come all!
Now gather! Now sing!
For this is the Day of the King!

No Shot Was Ever Heard

No shot was ever heard around the world.
In fact, in all of human history
Only two sounds have been heard around the entire world.
The first:
A newborn baby's cry, saying, "It is begun."
The second:
A young man's dying cry, saying,
    "It is finished."

*nce in every universe*
Some world is worry-torn
And hungry for a global lullaby.
O rest, poor race, and hurtle on through space—
God has umbilicated Himself to straw,
Laid by His thunderbolts and learned to cry.

Calvin Miller

Acknowledgments

The editor and publisher have made every effort to trace the ownership of all copyrighted material and to secure permission from copyright holders of such material. In the event of any question arising to the use of any material, the publisher and editor, while expressing regret for inadvertent error, will be pleased to make any necessary corrections in future printings.

Handels's Messiah by Philip Yancey, exerpted from "Hallelujah!" *Christianity Today* (December 15,1989, pages 30-33): used with permission.

Walter Wangerin, Jr., "A Psalm at the Sunrise" and "A Christmas Story," *The Manger is Empty*, Harper San Francisco, © 1989: used by permission.

Calvin Miller, "Anthem of the Star," *The Legend of the Brotherstone*, Harper San Francisco, © 1985: used by permission.

"Announcement": reprinted from *Postcard from the Shore*, ©1985 by Luci Shaw. Used by permission of Harold Shaw Publishers, Wheaton, IL.

"A Celibate Epiphany" and "Star Song": reprinted from *The Sighting*, © 1981 by Luci Shaw. Used with permission of Harold Shaw Publishers, Wheaton, IL.

"Under the Snowing," and "It is as if infancy were the whole of incarnation,": reprinted from *Polishing the Petoskey Stone*, © 1990 by Luci Shaw. Used with permission of Harold Shaw Publishers, Wheaton, IL.

---◇---